Thanks Be for These

Also by Richard S. Gilbert

In the Holy Quiet
How Much Do We Deserve? An Inquiry in Distributive Justice
The Prophetic Imperative: Social Gospel in Theory and Practice
In the Holy Quiet of This Hour
Building Your Own Theology (Volumes 1, 2 and 3)

Thanks Be for These

Meditations on Life and Death

Thanks Be for These reminds us we are creatures
who depend on a world we did not make,
and challenges us to be worthy.

Richard S. Gilbert

iUniverse, Inc.
Bloomington

THANKS BE FOR THESE
Meditations on Life and Death

iUniverse books may be ordered through booksellers or by contacting:

iUniverse
1663 Liberty Drive
Bloomington, IN 47403
www.iuniverse.com
1-800-Authors (1-800-288-4677)

ISBN: 978-1-4759-7319-8 (sc)
ISBN: 978-1-4759-7320-4 (ebk)

Printed in the United States of America

iUniverse rev. date: 01/25/2013

For Joyce, my wife of 51 years,
for whom I am grateful beyond all telling

Contents

Preface

I was sitting in a church sanctuary one Sunday afternoon listening to a string quartet. The space was spectacular, the sound was glorious, the moment was serendipitous and I jotted it down. All the rest is commentary on these four simple words.

Gratitude is at the heart of the religious experience, fundamentally a spiritual act. We are grateful, in the first place, for being itself. Everything else is a bonus. My gratitude is for life, not in the philosophical abstract, but in the existential concrete—for the details that make it worth living despite our finitude and the inherent messiness of existence.

These meditations share something of this spirit. While writing for public worship, I found the very act a personal spiritual practice. So these reflections are both public and private—public in our shared humanity, private in personal reflection on gratitude for life.

There is an almost desperate quest for spirituality in our time. The "nones" (who claim no religious community) are spiritual, but not religious. Gurus abound; quick fixes are everywhere. There is need for us to challenge ourselves to dig deeply into the meaning of our lives. These reflections on gratitude place the responsibility squarely on us—where it belongs.

I write from the perspective of a mystical religious humanist, seeking to merge the intellectual, the emotional and the spiritual. Far from offering "seven (or more) steps to internal peace," they reflect the ambiguity of life and urge us to make the most of it.

Thanks Be for These is in two sections. The first is a series of reflections on the fundamental human response of gratitude, which has been called the basic religious gesture. Their essence is captured in that respelling of a familiar word by a ministerial colleague who coined the term. This section is entitled "Thanksliving."

The second part consists of meditations written for memorial services when I sought to help families move from grief to gratitude for the life of their loved one. Some of the most meaningful moments of ministry come from helping people deal with life's finitude. These are life-affirming moments for which I am grateful. It is entitled "Gratitude in Grief." Thanks be for these.

Richard S. Gilbert
January 2013

Thanksliving

This first section of *Thanks Be for These* is described by a simple change of letter in a familiar word. I first encountered thanksLiving in the writings of a ministerial colleague who used the word in a ThanksGiving sermon. I was intrigued by its meaning then—and now.

As I reflect on more than fifty years of ministry, I am mindful of the many blessings that have been mine by virtue of having served several congregations peopled with amazing souls. I have also become aware of how very fortunate it is to have lived these years in good health and in good spirit.

Who am I to have deserved such rich experiences? Who am I to have enjoyed the beauties of nature and human nature for so long? I conclude that these are not benefits which I have "earned" in any moral sense of the word. They have simply surrounded me as I have lived. Theologians call it grace.

The following meditations, then, are about gratitude and living so as to merit the good we have experienced. They begin in thanksgiving and end in thanksliving.

Thank You

Thank you.
To what or whom I address the words I do not know.
I only know I must speak them.
If no one else hears, no matter.
I need to hear them for myself.

Bubbling up from some hidden well within
They come unbidden.
Blessings have come to me beyond my deserving,
This I know.

To be sure there are always moments of pain.
There are times I curse my fate and condemn my lot.
Life from time to time seems—IS—unfair.
My burdens often seem to outweigh my blessings.
All this I know.

Still, there is always the gift of life.
Always there are beauty and joy and meaning
Lurking beneath the blanket of depression and despair.
Always there are those who lift me.
Always there are lessons to be learned.
Always I would rather be than not.
Thank you.

January First

We have a new trial of time,
A year by fear yet untrammeled,
A decade by anxiety not yet stained,
A time to measure, make or mar.

And Judgment Day is every day,
And the Divine Judge is as near at hand
As we ourselves—
We, the ones on trial,
We, the accused, the judge, the jury,
Prosecution and defense
Rolled into one person, one people of earth.

We have a new trial of time.
May history judge us worthy.
May our progeny embrace us in pride.
May we learn to live with our amazing possibilities
And our incredible limitations
In courage and joy.

Carving Out a New Year

We stand before the new year as a painter before a blank canvass,
As a sculptor before a mass of stone,
As a composer before music paper with only lines and staff,
As a dancer before the movement begins.

To be sure, we have painted canvasses before;
We have carved out the shape of other years;
We have written other notes in time gone by;
We have moved through other hours.

But this is a fresh canvass,
Ready to receive colors never before imagined.
This is a new block of stone
Ready to be shaped by the chisel of mind and body.
This is a bundle of notes
Waiting to be arrayed across the beckoning page.
This is an open space
Waiting to host new steps and spins.

What are we to make of these colors we hold in our hands?
What are we to shape from this block of allotted time?
What melodies and harmonies will we create for the first time?
What movement will define the space once more granted to us?

What are we to make of this wonder while it is ours?
We tremble before the possibilities.
We feel anxious before the freedom given us.
We are apprehensive in the face of the new year.

Knowing all this, let us begin anew, with fresh courage to do and be.

The Earth Abides Forever

The seasons come and the seasons go,
But the earth abides forever.
The cold-whetted wind blew autumn from my mind,
The white snow whipped across my landscape
And reminded me of the changing seasons.

Another transition, paying no attention to the calendars,
Simply doing what it had to do to follow Nature's law.
The seasons are capricious here;
They come and go without warning;
They flaunt our human artifacts and devices;
They remind us of our finitude
And call to mind our dependence.

There is a strange beauty in their passing,
Something mysterious in the subtle or not so subtle
Changing of the guard.
The seasons seem indifferent to us
Who, after all, are in charge here, aren't we?
They act as if they do not need our permission to be or not to be.

It is a humbling reminder of irresistible forces
Meeting immovable objects
With inexorable persistence.
And we, with our little lives, tossed into this playground of Nature,
Strutting importantly about our business,
Try to learn to play our small part within the larger drama
In which we find ourselves.
The seasons come and the seasons go.
So do we.
But the earth abides forever.

Praise the Softness of Things

In the gentle joy of this time and season,
We praise the softness of things:
Soft snow as it tumbles down from an unseen source,
Or is driven by an invisible power across our path;
White snow as it embraces the earth
As a mother caresses her new-born.

It is not all gentleness, this time and season.
Mother Nature goes her winsome way with no thought of us,
Carving out new shapes, painting new forms,
Sounding a new song that leaves us forever guessing.
Wars do not cease in this gentle time of year,
Nor is violence forbidden to walk our streets.
Anger takes no holiday.

Yet, something gentle happens if we let it.
We pause to catch a snowflake on our sleeve
And admire its beauty for a fleeting instant.
We pause to kindle a fire without thought of hard efficiency.
We look for candlelight where we can find it.
We praise the softness of things.

Ordinary Magic in a Striving World

We are forever seeking release from the cares and frets of the world.
The world is too much with us—
Battering our psyches,
Flaying our spirits,
Wearying our souls,
Harrying our existence.

Meanwhile, Nature goes on, weaving its magic
While the world strives ceaselessly.
The seasons unfold as they should,
One following upon another,
Each with its special flavors and colors,
Sights and sounds.

In the noisy streets of this our time,
May we welcome the quiet blanket of white snow.
In the midst of confusion and complexity,
May we embrace the simple beauty of the snowflake.

Let us never be too busy with our lives
That we fail to pause and consider
The ordinary magic played on Nature's stage before us.
Let us stretch our cramped spirits to the heavens,
Reach out our stiff hands to catch a falling snowflake,
Bearer of intricate, delicate patterns,
And symbol of marvelous mystery.
It is such ordinary magic.

The Peace of a Winter Night

Welcome into the blessed peace of this night.
Be silent before the mystery in which we move.
Let us slow the beating of our hearts;
Let our breaths be measured;
Let our minds cease their mad dash to and fro.

May we center ourselves in this time and place,
Envision for a moment the peace of a winter night.
It is calm; it is still; points of stars prick the darkness;
The moon hovers in its arc above us.
Nothing stirs. There is no sound. There is peace.
We are enveloped in a deep darkness
That seems to have no end.
We rest in its grace.

Let our hearts be as the peace of a winter night.
May its calmness pervade us and its stillness quiet us.
May beacons of light point the way.
May the darkness sustain us in our going out and coming in.
May the memory of the moist, mystical night air
Be with us, now and forever more.
May we be blessed with the peace of a winter night.

Richard S. Gilbert

Impatient to Get Our Lives Started Again

In this holy season of the turning year
We are impatient for the spring to come.
Long dark days, plunging temperatures, falling snow
Have postponed our anticipation of soft breezes
And sunny skies and warm weather.
We have grown impatient with Mother Nature,
Even angry at the pace with which she ushers in a new season.
We are impatient for spring to be here—in truth—in fact—
Not just in calendar.

It is like that with our lives.
We are impatient for our lives to begin again;
Eager to get past our cold encounters with one another;
Ready to move beyond the failures and frustrations of gloomy days.
We anticipate a better time yet to be.
It seems the slowness of the season mirrors our languishing life.

Perhaps we should learn the patience of the earth.
It turns slowly, steadily, yet its seasons come and go
Somewhat as they please, but come and go they do.
May we come to enjoy each season of the soul as it is,
Not being too impatient about the next season,
Not being too eager for this time to pass away,
Not being too preoccupied with the time to come,
And thereby ignoring the time that is at hand.

We are impatient for spring to come;
We are impatient for our lives to begin again
In this holy season of the turning year—
the patience of the passing seasons' ritual.

On Sacred Listening

If you listen, you can hear the earth breathe.
It breathes through bugled bird-songs in the crisp morning air;
It breathes through hesitant buds about to break out;
It breathes through the brave persistence of the grass;
It breathes through the growing gush of water in the streambed;
It breathes through subtly-warming solar rays.
If you listen, truly listen, you can hear the earth breathe.

There are noises that can drown even the earth out:
The crude sounds of our engines fired into their work;
The rude sounds of forgetful folk who will not listen;
The raucous sounds of human commotion and contention;
The absurdities that distract us from the breathing earth;
The important work and words that stuff our ears.
But if we listen, really listen,
Earth's breathing will make us forget even these.

It is time again for sacred listening,
For putting our ears to the earth to catch its pulsing beat
As it puts to shame all our futile endeavors to run the cosmos,
Reminding us we are the creatures of earth, not its creator.
We only hope that our noisy breathing in and out
Will not drown out the chorus of creation
Which sings to bless us each turning season of the year.
The vernal choir is subtle in sound;
It does not insist we listen.
We always have a choice.
If you listen, you can hear the earth breathe.

A Walking Meditation in the Woods

My mind was too full
Of worries and plans and things to do.
My head ached, as did my back, to say nothing of my soul.
My heart was closed.
I could not hold the abundance of life.

My ears could not hear the sounds of spring.
My mouth too full of words to speak.
My hands too full of work to do.

I took myself away for a walk in the woods
Which surround my cathedral and my shrine,
My prison and my workhouse.

The air was cool, but not cold, rare and refreshing.
The birds had found voice and the sky was blue,
Interrupted by clouds adding depth to the view.
The ground was now firm underfoot.
Green was forcing its way everywhere.
Colors—gold and blue and rose—competed for attention.
It was too beautiful to bear.
Life was too intense—too good—too beautiful
To be believed.
Yet there I was on a walking meditation in the woods.

Spring Housecleaning of the Soul

Julian Huxley wrote: "It is of the greatest importance that humanity should now and then take out its beliefs for spring cleaning."

Not a bad idea.

May I purge myself of coldness of spirit that warm spring breezes may thaw my soul;

May the debris of wrongs unforgiven be gathered and discarded so I can start anew;

May slowness of spirit frozen by the cold be quickened to every fresh possibility;

May the song that has lingered too long in my lungs be released by twittering choruses;

May the grime of mistakes made be rinsed from my mind with the springtime waters of self-forgiveness;

May the dust of the exhausting journey be wiped from the furniture of my life so that it gleams again;

May my beliefs be taken out for a spring housecleaning of the spirit.

Spring Won't Take "No" for an Answer

We move in miracle this spring and Easter day.
Life is straining to change brown to green,
To warm the air we breathe,
To fill our nostrils with fresh fragrance.

We, the skeptical ones, know it is never so simple.
Green comes slowly, painfully, painstakingly, in its time.
Great northern winds can cut us to the bone
Even as we prepare the house of our spirit for spring.
Nonetheless, we make ready to be surprised by spring,
Lying restless within us, despite chill of body and soul.

Winter has reminded us that life must end in death,
That there are times of barrenness and loss
Which cannot be denied, only endured.
Yet we know the winter, as the spring, is not forever.
Always there is change—the changing of the seasons—
The changing seasons of the self.
Always there is the patience of the grass,
The cautious courage of the flowers,
The undaunted human spirit, ready for what may come.
Spring won't take "no" for an answer.
Neither should we.

Celebrating Brave Persistence

This Easter morn we celebrate human courage:
To call to mind in song and story one man's life and death;
To remember treasured words and unforgettable deeds;
To recall the power of one person to change the world;
To cherish all prophets of the human spirit who inspire us;
To take on something of their will and wisdom.

We sing praises to the brave persistence of the earth:
Year after faithful year the earth returns from its hibernation,
Blossoms burst forth as if signaled by some cosmic program
Of which we are but vaguely aware, and understand imperfectly.

Can it be we mortal souls take our cue from the immortal earth?
Can it be that we finite creatures try to imitate the infinite?
Can it be that we puzzlers over life's purpose
Seek to find the meaning of it all in the earth ball on which we live?

Can it be that in unraveling the mysteries of the earth
We descend into the depths of our own spirit?
Ascend to the heights of our own soul?
Can it be that this gigantic ball whirling through space
Becomes a laboratory of learning for mind and heart?

Can it be that the resurrection of the earth in spring
Reminds us of the immortality of the human enterprise
Which includes, and transcends, every last one of us?
May we learn to celebrate the brave persistence of the earth
And take into ourselves the courage of new beginnings.

Easter Is Paradox

Easter is paradox.
It is the leap over the chasm
Between life and death,
Between victory and defeat,
Between joy and sorrow.

Easter holds together reality of crucifixion,
And myth of resurrection,
The Jesus of history and the Christ of faith.

Those who lose their lives for others
Will be saved.
Those who save their lives for self
Will be lost.
Love is real only when we give it away.
Love hoarded melts as inevitably as spring snow.

"In the midst of winter, I found there was,
within me, an invincible summer." (Albert Camus)

Easter—I Hope He'll Be Remembered

I hope he'll be remembered.

Obscured by centuries of violence,

Clouded by countless creeds,

Dissected by a thousand scholars,

Preached from a million pulpits,

Mouthed by a billion lips,

Crucified by willful distortion

And innocent ignorance,

I hope he'll be remembered

In simple, unadorned humanity.

The Cup of Beauty

We come together as rivers seek the sea,
Bringing with us the waters of the earth.
We begin as tiny springs in far off places,
Gathering strength as we plunge down rough ravines,
And flow through peaceful valleys.

Always there are other living streams that join us,
Flow through us, sharing their strength.
Then ultimately all of us flow into the Great Ocean of Being.

We are like the waters of the earth;
We seek the peacefulness of a still, glimmering lake;
We search for the strength of the raging river;
We long for the freshness of the mountain spring.

And so from the springs and streams, lakes and oceans,
We commingle these waters in a cup of beauty.
We pour out the moments of our lives
Into a container that gives them shape and substance.
Knowing we are part of that Great Ocean of Being,
We treasure those fragile droplets that belong to us.

Here and now we give thanks for the cup of beauty
That is ours to create, ours to behold, ours to enjoy.

Spirit of the Wind

There is nothing more refreshing than the feel of a brisk wind on the face.

It helps if I am at the same time watching sunset over a lake—
The sky peach, purple, red, gold, blue, white, and orange at the same time.

It helps if the same wind that refreshes my face and cleans the air
Also takes me sailing across that narrow bounding main.

But the wind—what is there about the wind?

We cannot see it—only feel it—only observe what it does.
It has power, unseen power, a power that re-invigorates,
That cools on a hot day, that foretells a change in the weather—outer or inner.

The wind reminds us that the most powerful things are hardly tangible.
Their existence we doubt not.
Their power is not in question.

So it is with us. So may it be with us.

I could not touch the wind, but it touched me, and that was all I needed.

On Turning a Corner

As we approach the autumnal equinox, I turn to the words of Albert Camus for inspiration: "On certain mornings, as we turn a corner, an exquisite dew falls on our heart and then vanishes. But the freshness lingers, and this, always, is what the heart needs. The earth must have risen in just such a light the morning the world was born."

Earth turns a corner as it eases us from summer into autumn. Gently, imperceptibly, we are ushered into yet another subtle changing of the seasons. In our rapid gate we scarcely notice the early changing of the sumac leaves to crimson, the first formations of geese winging their way south, the fresh nip in the nighttime air.

We turn the corner of the year and behold ever-fresh beauty. We are greeted with sights and sounds so familiar, yet so eternally new, in each journey of our planet around its star. It is as if the world were born anew each year—time after time after cosmic time.

It happens with our knowledge, but without our control. We can merely observe these repetitions of universal order. There is nothing we can do to stay or promote the process. We are simply awe-struck observers as the earth turns the corner of the year.

We turn our own corners of the spirit—mend old mistakes—behold new vistas—imagine new adventures. Around each corner is a reminder of the eternal journey we are privileged to share. Each day is a fresh beginning, each hour a time for rebirth, each moment we spend on earth is a miracle—as we turn the corner.

Gifts of Necessity and of Choice

We pause before the miracles of this hour to consider giving and receiving,
A pattern writ deep in our hearts.
Always we are receiving gifts of the ordinary and extraordinary:

Trees give up leaves to nourish the earth on which we depend;
Fall gives up its colors to the blander hues of the cold season;
The fields yield up their produce to feed our bodies;
The sun shares its warmth through the cold reaches of space;
The clouds gently water the parched earth for our benefit;
The birds chorus their unbidden songs from tree and sky;
The earth provides everything needed for our survival;
The heavens themselves cast a sparkling shower of light for our enjoyment;
Time gives us hours and days and years to spend as we see fit;
Space gives us a place to be in the pointless universe;

The Great Life Process provides for us unparalleled blessings:
The privilege of living and the mystery of dying.
Creation gives and we receive.
Always we are receiving—is that a surprise?
Some gifts must be given—there is no choice.
The givers have no say in the matter.
We do.

What gift shall we bring before the altar of Creation?
What gift shall we give?
It is a simple gift.
We call it thanks-giving.

On the Cusp of the Year

We need to pause in quiet thoughtfulness on the cusp of the year,
The turning of the seasons.
As we pause in meditation,
The great natural rhythms move from summer to autumn,
In the never-ending, never-changing carnival of nature.
The colors begin to change from green to gold and red and yellow,
Creating new tapestries for our eyes.

At this cusp of the seasons we, too, would change.
We would take every opportunity to create a new season in our lives.
In this time of seasonal shift we remember we, too, can change.
We can claim the better angels of our nature.
We can forgo those habits of the spirit of which we are not proud.

At this cusp of the season, our lives are at a turning point,
As each season, each day,
Presents a clean slate on which we can write the story of our lives.
Let this hour, this day, this season be the beginning.

The Freshness of a Fall Day

In the whirling dance of the seasons
We savor the freshness of a fall day.
Unbidden it comes with blinding sunshine
Against a true blue sky that is infinite so far as we know.

Through no merit of our own we breathe in deep gulps of an air so crisp
Our tired bodies find new energy
Quite beyond our power even to comprehend.
The beginning dabs of color on green hillsides
Move us to marvel that we live in such a world.

It is as if all the powers of truth, goodness and beauty
Have conspired to grant us this one perfect day.
There will be other days—
Days drab with fog;
Days wet with rain and heavy with snow;
Days that chill our spirits to the bone;
Nondescript days that test our mettle to endure.

But we who have experienced this singular day,
We who have been embraced by such loveliness,
We who have been privileged to be alive in such splendor,
We who have known the incomparable autumnal miracle,
Will savor forever the freshness of a fall day.
And it will be enough.

Richard S. Gilbert

The Moon Is Full—
Autumn Nights Grow Longer

"The moon is full, the autumn nights grow longer." (Wei Ying Wu)

And we, children of the earth, prepare ourselves for dark and cold.
We grumble, perhaps, at the changing of the seasons.
We miss the warm sun, the gentle breezes and long, bright days.
We regret their going, as the passing of old friends.

Riding the spinning globe, we are propelled into a new time—
One that braces us for what is to come of seasons and of life.
The colors of autumn salve our hurts and we rejoice in their beauty.
The brilliant hues of red and orange, gold and green
Play together in a riot of color that defies the painter's pallet.
The fresh air invigorates us as we inhale—too delicious for words,
And new energy permeates our seasonal being.

We who live in temperate climes count ourselves fortunate to be
Alive in such a time and such a place.
We know the changing fortunes of existence
Because we know the changing of the seasons.
The only permanence in nature or in life is change.

While something in us clamors for stability, for sameness
In the deeper regions of our being,
We know we are made for change.
Boredom is worst of all—the steady sameness of no growth.
We can never stay in the same place of the spirit.
Something in us needs to move on.
The full moon in the lengthening autumnal night
Moves inexorably across the gray sky to remind us.
Wax and wane; wax and wane. It is the story of existence.
May we behold this beauty while it is here.

Grace for Thanksgiving

In the holy quiet of this Thanksgiving Day we pause to express simple gratitude.

While the world about us abounds in noisy confusion,
We give thanks for this time of peaceful quiet.

While we are tempted to complain about the difficulties that beset us,
We give thanks for the gifts that bless us.

While the world is too much with us,
We give thanks for the wisdom of the spirit to guide us through.

While we acknowledge hurts of body and soul,
We give thanks for the healing power of the universe.

While we suffer times of loneliness,
We give thanks for friends and family in time of need.

While there is much to make us sad this day,
We give thanks for all that makes us glad.

May the food we are about to eat be blessed to our use,
And may we be blessed to the service of humanity.

I Am Grateful

For the chill of an autumnal morning,

Reminding me I am alive,

I give humble thanks.

For the warmth of community against the cold indifference of the world,

I raise grateful hands.

For the grace of the sun setting quietly on a still lake and rolling hills,

I say thank you.

For a past that I have not yet forgotten though it recedes all too quickly,

I give glad thanks.

For the present that I can grasp, nettles and all,

I utter a prayer of praise.

For an unknown future that both tantalizes and threatens,

I am grateful.

Gratitude beyond Deserving

In this Thanksgiving season we pause
To give gratitude for that which is beyond our deserving,
The many graces of life which are ours,
Not because we have earned them
But simply because we are fortunate enough
To be here now, in this time and place and company.

Always we wonder if we get what we deserve,
If our labors will bring just recompense,
If our endeavors will be rewarded,
If our life projects will be completed.

Often we are saddened because we do not receive
As much as we believe we deserve,
That we have been unfairly treated by others—by life itself.

In this time of gratitude let us remember
All those things we have not earned;
All that blesses us beyond any merit of our own;
All the pleasures that come without effort;
All the joys that come to us when we are unaware;
All the beauty which greets us that we have not fashioned
But are privileged to enjoy.

May we come to understand that life is not a balancing act
That requires easy calculations of reward and merit.
Life is a mystery deeper than all our attempts to understand.
It is a miracle we are privileged to share with one another.
Let us be grateful for that which is beyond our deserving.

Thanksgiving into Thanksliving

We are the lucky ones, blessed beyond all telling
By the grace of living in a cosmic order
Whose mysteries both baffle and intrigue us;
By the bounties of the earth, our planetary home;
By the kindness of friends and strangers alike
Who gladden our hearts, celebrate our joys, heal our hurts;
By the fortunate circumstance of being born in a land
Of abundance and freedom.

How easy to forget our good fortune,
To assume our plenitude is etched into the very nature of things;
That our plenty is written somewhere out there in the stars;
That we have deserved all that we have;
That our virtue alone has brought us these untold gifts.

In this time of thanksgiving may we be humble
Before the great wonder of our bounty;
Before the needs that cry out to be met;
By those not as fortunate as we.

In this season of gratitude may we take on strength
To use our gifts for greater giving to those in need;
To serve others from the overflowing blessings we enjoy;
To transform our thanksgiving into thanksliving.

Christmas: The Blessed Hush

In the blessed hush of this season we settle down.
We close off from our minds the noises that jangle our nerves.
We open our ears and our hearts to ancient music that both soothes
And sustains us.

How we long for these few moments of quiet,
Away from workaday things,
The incessant ringing of the phone,
The steady hum of the computer,
The crackling of electronic machines which will not let us be,
The constant buzz of *important* talk.

For a time we repair to a quieter world of the spirit
Where life is not a matter of getting things done;
Where life has to do with being alive in this moment.
There the experience of listening to story and song
Captures our notice and commands our attention.

To be sure we are about important things,
Our work in the world can be done by no one else.
We are a vital cog in the great scheme of things.
Just for a moment, let us put aside such important matters
And listen to angel songs and prophet voices.
Let us allow ourselves into the magic world of poetry and legend
Which speaks a truth escaping our daily notice.
Even as the cold penetrates our bodies
May we be warmed by the spirit of love.
Even as icy winds chill us to the very bone
May we be warmed by a rebirth of our love for one another.

In the blessed hush of this time, may we listen to the stirrings of our
Innermost selves and meet and greet them anew.
Hush. Hush.

A Mood of Expectancy

The earth has turned once more in its accustomed way,
And again our footsteps quicken.
Our voices are raised in familiar chorus.
The sights and sounds of Christmas
Greet our eyes and ears,
Almost as if we had never seen or heard them before.

There is a mood of expectancy.
What we are to expect, we do not know.
The least surprises are hidden beneath bright paper
And graceful ribbon.
The great surprises are the magic that happens
Whether we seek them or not.

There is a mood of expectancy.
The beauty is we do not know what to expect.
Tomorrow is an open door,
An untraveled journey,
An untouched feast.

Christmas is like that——a mood of expectancy.
For out of the birth of the humblest babe
May come one of the great prophets of the human spirit.
And out of each of us, proud or humble,
May yet come truth and beauty and goodness we cannot now imagine.
Christmas is a mood of expectancy.

A Christmas Greeting

Merry Christmas to those who delight in the warmth of their friends and
family, and to those who face Christmas alone.

Merry Christmas to those who eagerly await the blessed day,
And to those whose memories are brighter than their expectations.

Merry Christmas to those whose spirits soar with the wonder of holy days,
And to those who are hurting all the more deeply for the joy around them.

Merry Christmas to those who celebrate Christmas in robust health,
And to those who hurt in body or spirit.

Merry Christmas to those who have had a splendid year and feast their eyes
on an open future,
And to those for whom the future appears even more bleak than the past.

Merry Christmas to those who celebrate their first Christmas this year,
And to those who count each Christmas precious because their days have
been long upon the earth.

Merry Christmas to this happy, hurting human family.

May we be joined in that mystic oneness which celebrates our joys and heals
our pain.

We Are Words in Nature's Poem

On this turning of the seasons,
This holy day and this holy time,
May we learn we are words in nature's poem.

It is an epic poem with grand scope and cosmic reach.
It is a poem of stars and seasons,
Heaven and earth, life and death.

And we are the words that help give
Rhyme and rhythm and meaning to the stanza
In which we find ourselves.

It is a fragment of a couplet,
Yet essential to the whole.
Without us it lacks completion.

May we be worthy words in nature's wide frame.
May we be grateful participants in the poem,
And may we celebrate its beauty, truth and grace.

On the Hinge of the Year

We are living on the hinge of the year, swinging from season to season.
There are moments of depression as we recall summer pleasures past,
And times of apprehension as we prepare for winter's problems.
We know there is little we can do about either.
We know Nature will keep unfolding as it should,
And her creatures will simply have to adjust.

We are living on the hinges of the years, too,
As we swing through our short seasons of being,
Marveling at the ever-changing view.
Every day is a hinge in our lives.
We keep turning, opening the door of each new day
Not really knowing what it will bring.
Sometimes our hinges are rough with rust,
And turning is difficult.
Sometimes our hinges turn with facile touch,
And we welcome what is beyond each new door.

There are times we would like to stop,
To cease turning,
To be able to hold the door still just for a moment,
To savor the day and the night of now.
In our wiser moments we know the turning will continue,
For we live on the hinge of the seasons of life.
May our turning be for joy.

The Earth Speaks

We live as dwellers on the earth,
Wondering at the meaning of our brief sojourn.
What can it mean that we live here, amidst star and cloud,
Rain and wind, heat and cold, life and death?
Is there some transcendent meaning in it all,
Or is our journey but what we make it mean?

We shout our question to the heavens and the stars shine,
Mystic, mute messengers of—what?
We pose our question to the trees and they stand stately, serene,
silent—why?
We call our question down the valleys and they echo our voices,
But speak not, nor do the mountains which cup them.
What can it mean?
We seek answers from our comrades,
And they, dumbfounded as we,
Shrug their shoulders in blissful, unabashed ignorance.

Do we ask too much of earth?
Do we demand too much of our cosmic habitat?
Do we expect too much of nature's impartial providence?
After all, the winds blow, the moon shines, the sun warms,
The rain nourishes, the earth turns—and we live.
What more can we ask?
What more can we demand?
What more can we want?

We are flung through space by mystic forces whose source we can never know;
We careen through time and space on an adventure with cosmic consequences;
We dwell upon an earth eloquent in its silence—and it is enough.

In Praise of the Ordinary

I lift my voice this day in praise of the ordinary:
The endless routines of living;
Life's everyday rituals;
The boring things we do to exist;
The monotonous getting up in the morning;
Eating, working, going to bed at night;
Moving to and fro to make a living,
Enjoying a life.

I celebrate the simple things,
The things to which we give not a second thought:
The miracle of breathing;
The act of eating;
The cadences of daily speech;
The sounds of nature as a simple backdrop
To our complicated lives.

I celebrate leaves falling from the trees
And snow falling from the skies;
The brave persistence of the grass,
And the sleeping flowers of the fields.

Enough, I say, of big things and great things,
And extraordinary things, and ultimate things.
I celebrate the ordinary.
I lift my voice in praise.

Inner and Outer Weather
(of the spirit)

It is time to consider the inner and outer weather of our lives.
We make much of the weather with which we must deal in this fickle clime.
We proudly endure what we can take in stride
And bitterly complain over that which we cannot.
It is a game we play.

But, consider the outer and inner weather of existence.

Our outer weather we experience daily:
Encounters with others;
Events in work or play, market or forum, city or countryside;
The machinations of a hectic world.
We make much of the drama of our lives as we parade across the stage.

What of our inner weather?
What of the meaning of the daily events which mark
Our going out and our coming in?
What do we make of what happens to us—or do we make nothing at all of it?
Our inner weather marks what is essential in us.

It signifies the workings of the spirit.
It measures the meaning of our lives.
It marks the rites of passage through which we move.
It celebrates those tiny triumphs of the soul we cherish.
It moves us to heights of ecstasy
And sustains us in depths of despair.
It shelters us in moments of loss
And supports us when we are sore distressed.
It enables us to endure and prevail
When life seems only to buffet and rebuff us.
It helps us understand the mysteries that surround us
And praise the majesty in which we live.

Behold our inner weather—the workings of the spirit.
May we embrace it, relish it, celebrate it all year round.

Ecology of the Spirit

We pause in the holy quiet to reflect on matters of the spirit:
As citizens of a nation;
As inhabitants of a planet;
As participants in a cosmos.

We are, ourselves, a universe.
We are a world.
We are an eco-system,
A complex system of thoughts and feelings,
A web of love and hates,
A matrix of anxieties and aspirations.

In this quiet time we take account of our inner ecology—
How we feel about the state of our lives;
What we think about the life we lead.
We consider well our ways and how we may mend them,
How we may restore order to our turbulent lives.

In these moments of reflection we seek balance.
We try to harmonize our lives with the earth
And those whom we meet upon it.
We seek to conserve our inner resources for what lies ahead;
To be good stewards of who and what we are;
To be sensitive to what we need to have;
To be, to do, to give.

May we find our own internal universe in tune
With stars and suns and moons in their cosmic swirl.
May we live in harmony with the inner ecology of our being.

Living on the Margins

We live on the margins of things.
We live on the borders of seasons, each struggling to cross over,
Confusing us with their spontaneous dance.

We live on the outer skin of the great earth ball,
Tenaciously clinging to precarious life.

We live at the cutting edge of history between a world that has died
And a world still struggling to be born.

We live on a marginal planet in a great galaxy on the cosmic periphery.

We stand always on the threshold of a new day,
Looking both back and forward.

We stand on the brim of the hill of the unknown,
Wondering what lies beyond.

We assemble on the verge of mystic cosmic forces we do not understand,
Which require our response.

We pause at the rim of a future we cannot
Yet envision in all its dimensions of pain and glory.

May we look well to the growing edge,
The moving line between what we have been
And what we aspire to be;
Between what we have done in sorrow
And what we anticipate in joy;
Between what we have failed to do
And what we hope to be.

We live on the margins of things.
Let us be grateful.
Look well to the growing edge.

In Praise of Pain

We gather ourselves in the peaceful calm of this moment
And in the healing presence of the Spirit of Life
To consider our lives as they are and as we want them to be.
We acknowledge our pain
And seek relief from its burdens.

Even as we do, we would speak a word in praise of pain.
There is always pain in our lives—sometimes less,
Sometimes more.
It is a condition with which we live.

When we are in touch with that pain
We know its teaching power.
While it casts a shadow over what we do,
It also grants us the sunshine of healing
And reminds us of those who share that pain with us.

Pain puts our lives in perspective.
We come to learn what is important, and what is not.
We grow in our capacity to comprehend the pain of others
And, sometimes, in our ability to help them.
Pain teaches us the hard lessons of our finitude,
Of our flawed nature, of the limits of life, as nothing else.

May we speak in praise of pain, and healing, and helping,
In the blessed calm of this moment
and in the healing presence of the Spirit of Life.

Love the World

LOVE the world, "big bang" and all.
Enter into the Milky Way with gratitude;
Shoot the stars gently, with awe;
And be glad you have a right to be here.

EMBRACE the earth
In all her terror and glory.
Sing praises unto her name.
Dig into her soil tenderly
And rejoice at the fruit in your hands.

ENJOY existence,
Life's categorical imperative.
Celebrate the life-long birthday party
Of one blessed by pleasure and pain alike,
Affirming in the end that life is good.

CREATE community,
For we are members, one of another.
Live in the unending charm of persons
Who people this world with us
Sharing the ambiguity
That is human living.

ACT as if it depends on you.
It doesn't, for no one can do it alone;
It *does* depend on us.
We are here to help one another
And the world—
Else what are we here for?

One Shining Day Makes
Worthwhile the Clouds

One shining day makes worthwhile the clouds—
Incandescent blue and green mingled with brown
Inspire me this singular day.
Time and weather and season conspire
To impose this magnificence upon me.

Whether I will or not,
Beauty penetrates me, permeates me,
Fills my callous spirit with life,
And I am drawn into the cosmic majesty
For a splendid instant.

Days of cloud and gray are with me yet.
There will be other than this shining day—
Days when my sullen soul will find no beauty in it at all;
Days when my spirit is bleak
And darkness clouds my horizon;
Days when nothing matters but the pain of being;
Days when nothing there is makes sense,
And joy is a stranger.

But this is a shining day:
Green and blue and brown
Paint my landscape lovely.
The winds of the heavens thrill by their touch.
My world is in order
And my soul is at peace.
There are no clouds that can take from me
The miracle of this shining day.

The Something Mores of Life

Today we would celebrate the something mores of existence:
There is something more to life than rising, eating, working, sleeping;
More than talking, listening, thinking, feeling;
More than seeing, hearing, tasting, smelling, touching;
More than mind can know or heart can feel;
More than getting and giving;
More than victory or defeat;
More than we can sense or fully explain.

Today we would celebrate the something mores of our lives:
There is the comforting rhythm beneath the daily routine;
The sense of being a treasured part of the human community;
The faith that there lies a power beneath all things that we cannot
apprehend with our senses;
The humility that with all our understanding
We are as children playing at the seashore of the infinite sea;
The wisdom that we are here not to get and spend
But to endow our lives with meaning.

There is the delight in being part of a mystery that is
Something more than our solitary life;
Something more than a single passage from birth to death;
Something more than we can fully express.

May we be ever open to the something mores of existence.
There is always, always, always—something more.

Living in the Grace of the World

In the sacred stillness of this moment
Pause to reflect on our place in a world we cannot fully comprehend.
Some are heavy-laden and seek strength;
Some are light-hearted and wish to celebrate;
Some are sorrowful and search for solace;
Some are happy and hope to share life's joys.

All wonder if we have deserved our lot in life—
If the rain falls upon us because of mistakes we have made
Or if the sun shines upon us because of the good we have done.
We are so caught up in the immediacy of our lives
We are tempted to forget the larger picture—
That we are but small pieces in the puzzle of existence,
That the web of cause and effect is complex,
That we often do not get what we think we deserve,
That people who are generous often suffer,
That people who are self-indulgent often prosper.

What can we do before the seeming indifference of the universe?
We can remind ourselves of the many graces of the world:
The steadiness of the turning earth beneath our feet;
The happy meeting of new friends when we least expect them;
The kindness of strangers when we are low;
The loyalty of those who stay with us in all seasons.
We live in the grace of the world.
Let us be grateful.

Richard S. Gilbert

For the Ambivalent Blessings

For the unabashed blessings of life we are grateful.

We would give thanks for life's ambivalent blessings:
For the blessings of middle age aches and pains we give thanks;
They remind us of healthier times past and the wisdom of endurance.

For the blessings of a botched and broken world we give thanks;
Its troubles help us transcend our smallness of self in service.

For the blessings of grief and bereavement we give thanks;
That we have loved enough to know the deep healing of tears.

For the blessings of quirky people we give thanks;
We discover anew the quirkiness that lies in us.

For the blessings of wild and wily weather we give thanks;
We know that such unpredictability is the best training for life.

For cosmic caprice with its random bursts of showing-off we give thanks;
We learn that beneath the routines of life there will always be surprises.

And so, for the ordinary blessings of life we give thanks this day.
For the ambivalent blessings that forever protect us from boredom
We are grateful.

The Unending Charm of Persons

Ridiculous they parade before us—the pitiful and powerful stream of
  humanity:

Polyglot—tall and short, brilliant and ignorant, good and evil,
Our cause and our curse;

Striding purposefully, wandering aimlessly, embarking on bold ventures,
  Cowering in apathy;

Believers and non-believers, the committed and the uncommitted.

With such as these are we doomed and destined to live our own drama,

Knowing the best and the worst in this world of peoplehood are with us,
  and in us.

It is us.

And rising above the pain and confusion, the din and danger, is the "sad
  sweet music of humanity" trying to make sense of the senseless.

Rising above all, for ears to hear and eyes to see,
Is the unending charm of persons,
The infinite variety of their sights and sounds and smells pervading all else.

The crude harmony of their voices, the rich textures of their bodies,
The strength of their limbs,
The total unpredictability and unrepeatability of their stories.

May our hearts never become so hardened,
May our eyes never be so blind,
May our ears never be so stopped that we blot from our consciousness
The unending charm of persons.

Richard S. Gilbert

Cheerleaders of the Spirit

Here we are, in the blessed peace of this place in time and space—
Athletes of the spirit running the race that is set before us.
For some the race has just begun and the spirit is full—
Zest and energy and strength abound.

For others the race is in mid-course and there is need for a second wind,
A restful pause, renewed resolve.

For others the race is near the end and there is need for the measured step,
The restful backward look on the way that has been run,
And still time to canter to the finish line.

In this moment of reflection and renewal
We take time to cherish the ultimate race we run—
That brief passage between birth and death we call life.
Living is so dear.

Here and now may we take our rest; here and now may we bind up our
Injuries; here and now may we learn to pace ourselves for what is to come;
Here and now may we learn to encourage one another
In the only race that really matters.

In this holy moment, may we learn to become cheerleaders of the spirit—
Urging each other on, shouting encouragement, reaching out our hands,
Celebrating our triumphs, consoling one another in loss,
Rejoicing in the privilege of running the most important race of all.

To Life!

Praise to the Spinning Earth

Praise, praise to the spinning earth!
Shout praise for the pounding seas!
Sound praise for the towering mountains!
Sing praise for the turning year!

Sound the trumpet, pluck the harp, sing alleluia
For the shining, splendid miracle of life.
Crash the cymbal, pound the drum
For the precious, pulsating surprise of being.

Praise ye the people, the many splendored people,
The young and the old, the happy and the sad
Who have come out from their habitations
To embrace this spinning earth.
Give praise and rejoice!
Give praise and rejoice!
Alleluia!

Spirit of Compassion

O Spirit of Compassion,
Enter our hearts, we pray.
Be with us in the hard hours.
Help us to be kindly this day.

O Spirit of Unity,
Help us enter into the pain of our neighbors.
Let us walk where they walk,
That we might speak a gentle word along the way.

O Spirit of Love,
Enlarge our sympathies toward all troubled folk.
Let us be generous of heart,
That we might forgive and be forgiven.

O Spirit of Thanksgiving,
Let us be grateful for hands that serve,
For those who give,
And for those who receive.

O Spirit of Life,
Let us walk together in our weakness,
That by treading the path together,
We may be made strong.

O Spirit of the Spheres,
Help us to face the mystery of being.
Secure us in the larger patterns we can trust,
And bless us this holy day.

The Life Force Within

Do you feel it? Do you sense it?
Pulsing within us at this very moment is the Life Force.

It beats rhythmically in our hearts, courses through our veins.
It informs our every thought, every feeling, every movement.

This Life Force existed eons ago,
Before the human experiment was even a gleam in the cosmic eye.

It was part of primeval ooze then,
Even as it is part of our human brain now.

We do not know its name—though many name it.
We do not know its direction—though we long to do so.

We do not know its destiny—though we are part of it.
We life-bearing creatures help shape its future,
Even as we celebrate its presence among us
And give thanks for its rich history.
We are bearers of the Life Force

It lives within us.
Be glad.

Transcendence

There is a beyond from which I have come,
Hidden in dark, moist mysteries of primeval mud
And the silence between the stars.

My past is shrouded in nameless men and women
Who peopled the earth before me.
The why of my being is lost in the
Answerless questions that bedevil my mind.

There is a beyond in which I live and move,
Inner recesses of the soul which reveal
Themselves at their own bidding,
Unaccountably breaking in upon the ordinariness—
Outer resources of heaven and earth
Which dwarf me by their vast complexity
And raise me up in simple ecstasy.

There is a beyond that beckons me
Into a wilderness of the soul.
I go in fear and faith
Knowing not what I will find,
Knowing only I must go into that beyond.

Praise unto that which is beyond.

We Are Bits of Starfire

There burns within each of us a sacred spark
Struck from some cosmic fire
Whose source we will never know.
Perhaps we came from the distant stars,
Vast whirling burning gases
Blazing in the black hole of space.

By what mysterious process are we here—
We who would gaze at the stars as stranger
When we are of the same stuff as they?
By what miracle are we born out of the Milky Way
In which we are but a peripheral part
And awe-struck observer?
Can we look at the stars and forget
That we are cast from the same elements in which they burn?
Can we gaze into the heavens and forget
That we are the commingling of heaven and earth
In a star-struck world?

It is no ordinary spark that ignites our being,
No ordinary fire that burns deep within,
No ordinary flame that flares
Between the twin nights of birth and death.
We who live are of the divine fire;
We who live and breathe are mysteries of the universe;
We who live and breathe and have our being are cosmic creatures.

We are sparks of the holy come to life.
We are bits of starfire.
May we nourish the flame within us;
May we let the light of our faith shine;
And may we pass on the torch to those who follow.

The Gift of Today

Life is measured in years while it is lived in days.

Life tales are told in generations of past, present and future,
While it is lived one day at a time.

The gift of life is not a gift of great sweeps of years but in the single day—
The day which we live now.

It is tempting to live off the capital of yesterday,
Or the anticipation of tomorrow,
But it is today that the hands of the clock measure the hours of our lives,
And it is the presence of time within us that tells its significance.

Why must we live in that can-never-again-be
Or the future-that-has-not-yet-come?

Why can we not look at the gift of today and fall on our knees in gratitude?

You Are Breath

Breathe. Breathe deeply . . . inhale . . . exhale . . . breathe.
You breathe not alone.
Hear the deep breathing in your own breast,
The breathing of your neighbors,
And know the whole of humanity breathes with you.
You are a column of air.
The air passes over your vocal chords
Issuing forth in speech and song.
Listen to the sound; listen to the melody,
And know the community of those who share word and music.

You are a snowflake dancing through the cold air,
Tumbling toward the earth with your myriad neighbors.
Feel the freedom of flight,
And know the beauty you create with your companions.
You are the air that envelops the earth—
Embracing a life-giving globe with your protecting arms,
Creating new patterns of weather and of clime,
Ever changing, ever washing the sky.
Feel the softness and know that you give life and breath.

Breathe. Breathe deeply . . . inhale . . . exhale . . . breathe.
Feel the air move up and down in your throat;
Behold the lovely sound of breathing creatures;
Sense the power that breathing slowly brings;
Embrace your comrades near and far.
And know where there is breath, there, too, is life.
Breathe. Breathe deeply . . . inhale . . . exhale . . . breathe.

"You Are Accepted.
Accept the Fact You Are Accepted. "

Paul Tillich

"You are accepted. Accept the fact you are accepted."
The universe has hurled you into being,
One among many infinite variations of cells that might have been.
It has created you unique among all creatures.
Cosmic codes translate into the person you are.
Natural forces from time immemorial have created you.
The universe accepts you for what you are.
You are a privileged citizen of a world blessed beyond all imagining.
The great globe spins and whirls to bring you
Sunshine by day and stars by night.
The earth ball favors you with changing seasons,
With air for your lungs, with food for your appetite,
With shelter for your body.
The world accepts you for what you are.
You are a creature of history,
Favored by the prophets and poets who have gone before.
The yearnings of men and women are the realities in which you live.
The wisdom of the ages is captured in the books you read.
The music of the spirit thrills your ears.
History converges on you now and here.
History accepts you for what you are.
The sanctity of your conscience is cherished by all.
Your spirit is free to soar as it will.
Your mind may move as it chooses.
There are no fetters on your faith.
One thing only remains, and that is hardest of all.
Accept yourself. You are accepted. Accept the fact that you are accepted.

Gratitude in Grief

I have conducted hundreds of funerals and memorial services, counseling with hundreds of grieving families who seek the meaning in the death of a loved one. It may seem strange to say it, but these experiences have been a blessing for which I am grateful.

Part of that good fortune is encountering very courageous and loving human beings. Those who grieve form a special company of those who share the pain of loss. They are driven to the deepest regions of their souls. It has been a privilege to know them.

Another part of this process of enabling grief has been learning about the lives of those who have departed. In most cases I have known them, but in preparing memorial services and eulogies, I came to know them much more intimately. The term "celebration of life" indicates my approach to helping their survivors appreciate their lives.

A final gift in ministry is having again and again the opportunity to reflect on my own mortality, the meanings which inform it. As they were leaving a memorial service, a veteran minister once said to a ministerial intern: "Each time I die a little." Doing this work extracts a certain energy, but it also energizes me for living the days remaining in my life journey.

And so, in these reflections, I express my gratitude for grief—the many powerful experiences, the opportunities to share life and death with my companions, and the urgency of living a life worthy of these several blessings.

To Acknowledge a Death

From time to time we gather together to acknowledge a death. We come also to celebrate a life and take that life into the guardianship of memory. We come together as family, friends and colleagues to share our loss and to rejoice in the memory of a singular life.

When a loved one dies, their friends and family gather together for many reasons. Just to be together, to feel the common experience of grief, binds us together in healing that men and women and children can do for one another. Just to look into each others' faces and see the common expression of hurt is balm to the spirit.

At such times the various religious faiths that sustain us separately, our different ways of looking at life and death, come together and cut across all creeds to remind us of the immortality of goodness and the value of a serviceable life. What at times seems to divide us, at such moments unites us in a common reverence for life.

And so we share our memories of them, hoping that in so doing we will heal our wounded spirits and transform our sadness into rich memories.

We form communities of human memory. We create for ourselves a living picture of them etched in love.

We gather to hear words of inspiration from the prophets and poets of humanity, to share memories and to deepen the meanings of our own lives as we face the future without them.

We cannot undo what has happened; we can together summon up the strength to face it in dignity and courage.

We form communities of human hope, knowing that even as we acknowledge death, life goes on and on.

We gather, not only to mourn a death but also to celebrate a life, seeking to distill the essence of what that life meant to us.

We Gather in Grief

We need to be together to share our sorrow when we lose a loved one, to remember a unique life, and to begin to prepare ourselves for the days and years ahead. It has been a long and hard journey. Our friend's journey, and their suffering, is over. Our journeys will continue—in sorrow, but also in thankfulness and in hope.

There is a painful emptiness in our lives that cannot be filled. We will carry something of that pain as we continue our lives without them. Yet we will also carry something of the courage and the dignity, the love and the grace, with which they lived.

We acknowledge in sadness the fact that their life has ended. This we know in our minds, but in our hearts the death of one we loved is hard to accept. We had known for some time that they would leave us, we have tried to be prepared, but the harsh reality of their death cuts us to the quick.

Memories Crowd upon Us

Memories crowd upon us as we remember the years that have passed:
Many high hopes envisioned;
Many blunders made;
Many blessings enjoyed;
Many dreams shattered.
In this moment of return we would reflect upon our lives.

Memories crowd upon us as we recall our days together:
Many joys unanticipated;
Many moments of undeserved beauty;
Many little unexpected graces.
In the sweet taste of our happiness
We savor what we would never yield.

Memories crowd upon us,
Shaping the self that tomorrow
Will re-enter the world of memory and hope.
Memories crowd upon us, sweet and bitter,
Friendships rekindled,
Indelible now, written on the tablet of the heart.

There are more moments to create in the world of today.
May the memories of yesterday and the hopes of tomorrow
Lead us faithfully through this day.

Unprepared for Death

It is especially hard to comprehend the death of one we loved, who not long ago was among us. It does not seem possible they are no longer living, they are so vivid in our memories. The stark truth of what has happened is nearly impossible to accept.

Nothing in life prepares us for death, even though we know it always hovers over us. Life is marked by risk and uncertainty from birth to death.

The death of a friend or loved one reminds us how fragile is the thread of life. Though life seems strong and will long endure, sharp shears of death can cut it before its time.

As the Japanese poet Buson put it so graphically: "Before the white chrysanthemums the scissors hesitate for an instant."

Richard S. Gilbert

Remembrance and Remembering

Two words,
Same root,
Different meaning.
Remembering is a simple act of recalling the past—
Its shape and lineaments and moments.
Remembrance, however, is quite a different matter.
Remembrance is recalling the past in a way
which inspires us to mold a future.

Remembering is easy.
Humans are remembering creatures.
We remember as regularly as we eat and sleep.
It is as natural as getting up in the morning
And going to bed at night.
It is an act of the mind.

Remembrance is hard.
It requires that the memory of the past
Guide our present and inspire our future.
Remembering is passive images coming into us.
Remembrance is active—
It catches up the memory and mixes it in
The alchemy of our lives
And we emerge from the process as new people.

Let us remember, of course—
We need to remember.
Let us also hold in remembrance those persons,
Those events, those experiences,
That have the power to transform our lives.
Then is embodied in us past, present and future,
All bound up in the transitory creatures that we are.

Why? A Question without Answer

We are inevitably torn with the question, why? Why do young people have to die before their time?

Why do bad things happen to good people?

We cry out in our bitterness. It is natural to do so. We do not want to accept what has happened. We cannot find any justice in it. With the poet we do not approve—we are not resigned.

In our wiser moments we know "why?" is a question without answer. We are not given to know the whys of life and death; they are bound up in mysteries whose depths we cannot fully probe.

We seek answers as people have before us, but in the depths of our being, we know we will not find out. It is simply not given us to know.

We can but give thanks for the precious time granted to all of us, realize as never before the treasured time allotted to each of us, and learn to use it wisely.

Tempted by Guilt

We are often tempted toward guilt at the sudden death of a loved one.

It is natural to wonder if we have done all we could to take responsibility for the life of another.

We can torture ourselves with the "ifs" of human existence until our dying day.

We need to remind ourselves that no one can take full responsibility for the life of another.

In the final analysis, each is responsible for his or her own life.

We can only share in that responsibility, acquitting those tasks as best we can.

We are not prepared, can never be fully prepared, for sudden and premature death.

But they died as they wished—with no heroic measures to prolong their suffering, with their "boots on" so to speak—fully engaged in life.

What more can we ask?

What more can we do?

"Given our best endeavor, the final result is not with us." (John Dewey)

Reflections on Facing Death and Life

Some see life as a process of tearing the pages from a calendar and throwing them away, always looking to the pages still intact—the future.

For me, life is a process of removing pages from the calendar and looking to those still intact.

But it also consists, not of throwing the used pages away, but filing them away as experiences, memories which can never be lost.

The life we live, all too brief, has its own validity, its own fullness, its own memories stored in the hearts and minds of those who love us for as long as they shall live.

And so what can we do in the face of death but let our tears flow freely, for in time they will dry and give birth to a smile.

What can we do but accept the hurt, for in time the hurt will be healed and we will be stronger than before.

In time the mourning will give way to loving memories; the hurts of the past will give way to a rebirth of our love for one another.

The emptiness in time will be filled both with memories of the past and times yet to be, for Life is greater than any individual life, and the Great Life Process does not tarry with death, but carries us on.

We can but choose to move with it, and in time learn again to enjoy it with all our being.

There Is a Healing that Happens

We pause before the mystery of life and death.

We know that death is as much a part of life as is birth; and yet a friend's death is unique to us—to those who shared their life and who now share their death.

In this moment of parting, then, we accept both the beauty and tragedy of life, its holiness and its limits, its joys and its sorrows, its yesterdays and its tomorrows.

However bereft we may feel at this moment, there is a healing that happens in the aftermath of death; there is a healing among family members and friends who have shared life's most intimate moments of joy and tragedy, love and loss.

The agony we feel will become sadness and the sadness will become loving memories which will fill our days as long as we live.

Have faith in the healing.

Reflection on Death

We are all amateurs in facing death.

Little in life prepares us for the finality of it all.

We face death with resignation, perhaps, or with rebellion.

Sometimes it comes as relief from suffering, sometimes with sudden tragedy, sometimes as both.

Always it comes into our lives as a kind of unreality—we cannot quite believe it is happening to those we love and to us.

We understandably seek release from our sense of loss and pain, some way to put it behind us.

But we know there is no way to do so. The pain must come and be experienced.

The sense of loss will be with us long after the sharp pain of parting is gone.

The feeling of emptiness and aloneness will not soon cease.

It cannot be any other way.

We have taken the risk of love, and when those we love die, it must wound our spirits.

We can but live through our grief, seek to heal our wounds and move ahead.

Walls that Guard Our Grief

If only we had more time to live,
More time to be with our loved ones
And properly prepare them and ourselves for their passing.
If only we had more time
To get ourselves together again.
If only the life clock would stop for a little while,
We could re-order our lives.
But time, as we know, waits for no one;
Life comes at us all the time.

At such times it is good to be reminded
We are not alone.
Not only are we companioned by those who
Share our ultimate fate,
But we are caught up in the healing embrace
Of the universe that sustains us.

Rejoice, then, in the walls that guard our grief:
     Walls of love against loneliness,
     Walls of laughter against sadness,
     Walls of life against death.

Rejoice in the mystery of the walls
That guard our grief
So that loneliness is absorbed in love,
Sadness is mingled with laughter,
Death becomes part of life.

The Universality of Death

We humans are strange and wondrous creatures, for we struggle against all the odds in what seems to be a losing cause. Death, we know, is inevitable. We face an experience as much a part of life as is birth. It is universal. It comes to all, to each, in the day or in the night. We know that death is part of life, yet we gladly take the risks of living.

We know we are but finite creatures in an apparently infinite universe. We know that we are but tiny specks in the great stream of history. We know our lives are but details in the great scheme of things. Yet we assert ourselves by living life as if it mattered, and, of course, it does. It is in the human details of the cosmic order that we find meaning.

We know that death is universal. No one escapes its inexorable coming. Yet, when it comes, it is always personal, always unique. Each life is a life unto itself, each life is different, each life carries its own joys and sorrows, its own triumphs and defeats. That uniqueness draws us together in grief and the rituals of parting.

We are comforted by realizing with the poet that "the deeper that sorrow carves into your being, the more joy you can contain." (Kahlil Gibran)

It is in the nature of human life that what has given us greatest joy when it is present also gives us greatest sadness when it is absent.

Ours is the joy in sharing another's life, and ours is the sadness of loss. Thus has it ever been; thus shall it ever be.

Life, Death, Time
and the Space between the Stars

(after Robert Ardrey in *African Genesis*)

On this cusp of the seasons we are moved
To consider life and death, time and the space between the stars.
This playful dance of winter and spring,
Howling winds of winter one day
And warming rays of sun the next,
Simply remind us we are not in charge of the seasons.
They trifle with us and go their own capricious ways.

We measure time in our precise human style,
Unable to imagine how brief is our time on the eternal clock,
How few our days on the cosmic calendar.
When we are at our best, we know time is short, precious,
And to be treasured as much fine gold.

We acknowledge our finitude.
We tell ourselves to be humble despite temptations to false pride,
To understand our tiny niche in the great scheme of things,
To celebrate the one and only life granted to us.

We come together as we float through the heavens,
Precariously perched on this whirling orb of earth
Unaware of our tenuous planetary position,
Content simply to be alive to enjoy the grand spectacle of Creation.

We come gladly to celebrate life and death,
Time and the space between the stars—
To drink in the mystery,
To partake of the beauty,
To relish the gift of life so graciously bestowed upon us.

Sometimes It Takes a Death

Sometimes it takes a death
To remind us of life:
To hear in a child's sobbing
A cry of love;
To change dog-eared cards and letters
Into holy writ;
To transform a gathering of loved ones
Into a sacrament.

Sometimes it takes a death
To remind us how short is life;
How infinitely precious
Are the commonplace deeds of love;
How treasured are the hours
of faith and friendship;
How strong are the bonds of caring community.

Sometimes it takes a death
To remind us life is good.

Richard S. Gilbert

Prayer on the Occasion of Death

In the holy quiet of our souls, we seek to find words of prayer when it is hard to pray. It seems the orderliness of the universe has become chaos; that our hopes have turned to despair; that our dreams have become nightmares.

In our wiser moments we know the death of one we loved can do this to us. Our minds tell us there is yet order in the universe; hope persists; we continue to dream. But our hearts will not so easily reassure us. Minds can make adjustments; hearts mend slowly.

So we pray that our hearts will hold no bitterness or guilt; that we may know and feel the quiet strength and order of the universe; that even engulfed in despair hope leads us on; that dreams rise again out of the ashes.

May a sense of relief come over us that suffering ends; may a sense of joy come over us as we remember our departed loved ones in the full vigor of their life; may a sense of hope come over us that they have given us so much for which to live.

May we learn the age-old lesson—out of death comes new life born in the memories of those we love; out of tragedy comes courage; out of grief comes strength; out of agony comes hope.

"And so may we be granted the serenity of mind
to accept that which cannot be changed,
the courage to change what can be changed,
and the wisdom to know the difference." (Reinhold Niebuhr)

Prayer for a Quiet Heart
in the Face of Death

In the name of all that is holy, we say our common farewell to a loved one. May we be granted a quiet heart and a strong serenity as we stand together before this unfathomable mystery of the universe.

May our hearts receive that peace which passes understanding; which sustains us in our darkest hour. May we have the courage and the faith once more to face the traffic of our days even as they faced their days, in faith, and hope and love.

May we be given strength that we may take up our lives more bravely, and seek to be more faithful in duty and more loving and helpful to others for the sake of those who are no longer with us. May we return to the daily round of duties more eager to be kind, as though in the presence of death itself we had learned to know the deeper meanings of life.

Thankful for those fine lives, in whose presence we walked the short years of earth, may we be more trusting and compassionate, now that they have been taken away.

Not forgetting the time that is past and the memory that is within, may we set our eyes and hearts to the future that beckons to us.

Prayer for a Person of Many Years

We pause in the silent mystery of life and death, time and space. In the holy quiet we reflect on the death of a person of many years. The life cycle has been completed and for this we are grateful.

May we be assured that this time is not so much one of sadness as of thanksgiving. Though the pain of losing one we loved over the long years is with us, we are deeply grateful for having shared them with our friend. In time our thanksgiving will overshadow the sadness and we will rejoice in their memory.

May a sense of relief come over us that they died only at the end of a long and fulfilling life. May a sense of relief come over us that their suffering has come to a peaceful end. May a sense of joy come over us as we remember them in the full vigor of their life. May a sense of hope come over us that their life has given us so much for which to live.

We Are by Them and of Them

There is a strength in men and women of age,
A strength unknown to youth.
There is a distilling—a sorting out of what is important
And what is not.
It is written on the face.

They know that which gives greatest joy also brings greatest pain.
But now "sorrow carves into our being" at loss of loved ones.
There is left a loneliness that cuts like a knife.

The elderly among us have lived through times and seasons.
They know the people's folly and fortitude and their own.
Theirs is the wisdom not of books, but of years—
The wisdom of loving and having been loved.
They know the patience of the years.
They know how universal is the life force that gave us birth,
But how particular are its manifestations.
The world is always the same, always different.

Brief interval between moments of birth and death,
Terminal disease, universally suffered—
A flash of light between two darknesses—
A mystery of spaces, vast and small—
A story beyond all telling—
A proud procession of men and women,
Great and small,
Who made the journey.
We are by them and of them.

Please Remember Me the Way I Was

Who are we anyway?

What is our essence?

Are we what we are now?

Or what we have been?

One day we will be at the last stage.

Let us remember, let everyone remember

That our lives are not simply what we are at the moment,

For good or ill.

We are the sum of the parts of an entire life.

Please remember me the way I was.

On the Death of a Child
(for the Children of Newtown, 2012)

The death of a child is always a crushing blow to the spirit. There is nothing that can soften the tragedy. There is only a slow, painful learning that life and death often are simply inexplicable. We stand in saddened humility before the great process of life and death some call God.

We are overwhelmed by shock and disbelief, as well as by love. The death of a child has a power to infuse us with a pain that seems infinite. Our sense of justice, of fairness, has been challenged and we need to respond to the tragedy that has brought us here. We acknowledge in sorrow this child who has been denied opportunity for a full life. The child is a melody unsung, a book just begun. We will never know how it might have ended.

Gradually, our pain will be transmuted into loving memories, and the loving kindness of those who have helped us through these troubled hours. We need to remember a child who spent so short a time among us. Even brief memories can be indelibly etched in our hearts. If so much that was precious can be lost before it became fully ours, let us cherish the memory that remains; and let us be the nurturers of things precious in the lives of others.

In our helplessness we wonder what we ought to do. What can we do before such a tragedy? We create community to share our sense of helplessness that we might give quiet expression to the sadness we feel. We gather with friends and family because we know not what else to do. We simply need each other. That is the lesson passed on to us from those who preceded us in so difficult a time.

The love we cannot give to this child we may be able to give to those who need it. May we be spared from frozenness of heart. May our compassion for others be deeper, our sympathy wider. May our bitterness melt away and may our sorrow teach us to be gentle. While the healing can never be complete, we live in faith that we will be able to embrace life all the more lovingly because of the death of a child.

Meditation on a Suicide

We are understandably shocked and saddened by our friend's tragic death. We do not know what to make of it, what to make of their final decision to take their own life, for to those who knew them, they could be a delightful person, though often troubled in spirit, knowing too much of turmoil and depression.

What burdens they bore we do not and will not know. We know only that no one can live another's life; no one can bear full responsibility for another's decision. It remained their choice. They died by that choice; we must learn to live with it.

That their death was such a shock to those who knew them suggests how little we really know of one another; how little we know of another's hurts; how limited is our capacity to help those in need. Perhaps, somehow, their departure from our midst may remind us to be gentle with one another, to take time to nurture friendship, to renew our sense of community.

Tragedy can bring out the best and the worst in us. It can plunge us into guilt and anger. We can ask why they did this to us. Tragedy also brings about a welling up of the community surrounding them, their friends and loved ones. It is a community transcending all our lives. It brings forth courage in loved ones, friends and colleagues who must reach down to the deepest reservoirs of strength to sustain and be sustained.

May our friend's last hours not obscure the meaning of their life—all those memories of joy they leave behind in those who loved them and lived with them through their too few years. May the tragedy of their death not obscure all the years of their life which enriched those about them. May our images of our friend not be trapped in those last hours of agony; rather may they reflect the totality of a life lived. May we have the wisdom to take that life whole. May we have the strength to love more fully those who need that love now that they are gone.

The Hourglass of Time

We live in the hourglass of time.
The sands of our lives pour relentlessly
Into the shapes of memory.
They cannot be stopped—only enjoyed.
The passage of time knows no holiday;
It slips away while we are too busy to notice.
On this fulcrum of the year we pause to consider time.
Time is, after all, what we have to work with—
It is the one resource that is finite and precious.
The sands of time are lovely to behold;
They sparkle in the sunshine
And gleam in the rain.
They are cool and firm in the hand—
Something of substance.
They are finer far than gold or silver.
Whether there are more grains of sand poured
Or to be poured does not matter.
We live in the hourglass of time
Shaping our memories and our destiny
In this gleaming glass
Whose loveliness we are privileged to behold.

Richard S. Gilbert

In the Midst of Life and Death

In the midst of life and death we would look at beginnings and endings.

How strange it is that in the presence of death our thoughts are of life—
The life of the beloved one now departed—
The history of a unique life—
The story of a person.

How strange that in the presence of death our thoughts are of life—
The life we lead, which one day will end—
The life that races on despite our efforts to slow the pace
Toward that one final and inevitable destination.

How strange that it takes a death to reflect upon a life—
That the ending of a human being
Means a beginning again for those of us who witness it.

We are both living and dying each and every day
The one and only life we are privileged to lead.

May we be thankful for the life-time we have.
May we give gratitude for those who have lived and died for us.
May we return thanks that we are given each and every day
A chance to begin again to live.
May this be our prayer in the midst of death and life—beginning again.

Between the Rising
and Falling of the Curtain

Between the rising of the curtain, birth,
And the falling of the curtain, death,
There is the precious and precarious play—
Of smiles through tears,
Of companions loved and lost,
Of death in life and life despite death.

Between the expectant hush of the audience
And its burst of acclaim or disapproval at play's end
We cavort back and forth upon the stage,
Now in the glow of the footlights,
Now in the shadows beyond the curtains.

All we can be sure of is that the curtain for us has risen,
And just as surely will one hour fall.

Death is to human life what the final curtain is to a play.
It gives to life form and substance.
It helps us understand the meaning of what has gone before;
To more fully appreciate the lives of those who have played their parts
And played them well.

Richard S. Gilbert

We've All Come Back

Inspired by poet John Holmes

We pause in the holy quiet to give thanks:
Another day has been granted us,
Another day is presented as a gift
Without our seeking,
Asking nothing of us in return—
Another day of living.

It is a small matter—a single day—a trivial occurrence
Measured against the length of a lifetime,
Measured against the span of human history,
Measured against the backdrop of eternity.

But this is our day—like no other day in our lives;
It is a day we can make or mar—
That we can spend wisely or waste foolishly—
That we can give or hoard.

Each day is like that—a blessing from who knows where,
An act of grace from who knows how,
A gesture from a universe whose origin and destiny we know not.
And so, this day, we've all come back to life.
We've all awakened from sleep to a day untouched.
We've all been granted a reprieve.

We're back, we've all come back.
We've all been granted the miracle of miracles—
A piece of time—minutes of opportunity—moments of promise.
We've all been granted a longer time to live and learn and love.

Epitaph
(Haiku)

I am not here now
But within and among you
My spirit lingers.

On Writing One's Own Obituary

He was born into the joy of human existence at precisely the one and only right moment for him.

He saw his life as a struggle for justifying the miracle of his existence.

He lived each day as if it were his last, seeking to crowd into it as much of the enjoyment of life as he could.

He had little patience for those who found life boring, who would fritter it away, minute by precious minute.

He died savoring life to the last delicious drop.

P.S. Do not take the above too seriously; one who cannot laugh at oneself is a bore and a fool,

Mark Twain wrote: "Let us endeavor so to live, that, when we come to die, even the undertaker will be sorry."

Lines for an Epitaph

There never was enough time for him
To be all he wanted to be,
But what he was, was enough.
He is one with the earth he trod,
He is one with the stars at which he gazed,
He is one with those he loved,
He is one with this world, our home.
On a long journey
What more do we have to share
Than just what we are?

Postscript

It is all over much too soon. Once we seem to be getting a handle on life, we come face to face with death. It is simply a shame that the wisdom I have now absorbed will go to waste with my demise. Not so fast. There is a time for reflecting deeply on what has gone before—a kind of summing up of the life enterprise. That in itself is sufficient justification for putting into words the distillation of one's learning.

The printed word, however, opens yet another possibility. It promises a kind of immortality by passing on those bits of meaning one has accumulated over the years, passing them on in something resembling a pattern of meaning.

I am agnostic about any conscious immortality, though my doubt suggests there will be none. However, my faith suggests to me that what I have experienced can never be erased in the Great Scheme of Things. Better yet, I can record something of the mystery and miracle of my existence for those who follow.

This is what I have tried to do. Whatever the result of this effort of faith, I can only summarize what I have learned in four simple words: "thanks be for these."

R. S. Gilbert

About the Author

Richard S. Gilbert is the author of meditations and books on social justice. A retired minister, he holds degrees from St. Lawrence University, Meadville/ Lombard Theological School, Starr King School for the Ministry and Colgate Rochester Crozer Divinity School. He lives with his wife Joyce in Rochester, NY, where they enjoy time with their three grandchildren.